Prepositional Words and Phrases for ESL Learners

STEPHEN LAU

Copyright © 2017 Stephen Lau
All rights reserved.
ISBN-10: 1539144569
ISBN-13: 978-1539144564

INTRODUCTION

Prepositions are words that indicate the *relationships* between various elements within a sentence. In formal English, prepositions are almost always followed by objects.

> e.g. The policeman shot (verb) the man (object) **with** (preposition identifying the man being shot) a knife.

> e.g. I put (verb) the pen (direct object) **on** (preposition indicating the position of the pen) the table (indirect object).

> e.g. I put (verb) the pen (direct object) **under** (preposition indicating the position of the pen) the table (indirect object)

Prepositional phrases always consist of the object and the preposition. Prepositional phrases can act as adjectives or adverbs. When they are used as adjectives, they modify nouns and pronouns in the same way single-word adjectives do. When prepositional phrases are used as adverbs, they also act in the same way single-word adverbs and adverb clauses do, modifying adjectives, verbs, and other adverbs.

Prepositional words and phrases are difficult, especially for ESL learners, because different prepositions may impart different meanings to the prepositional words and phrases. Even the same preposition may have different meanings to the same verb.

Break in: enter without permission; interrupt; train; get used to something new.

e.g. A burglar attempted to **break in** last night but without success.

e.g. Don't **break in** while someone is talking; it's rude!

e.g. The manager has to **break** the new employees **in** so that they may know what to do.

e.g. You should **break** your new car **in** before you drive on the highway.

This book has hundreds of prepositional words and phrases with explanations and examples, just like the ones illustrated above, for you reference. Improve your English with your mastery of prepositional words and phrases.

Stephen Lau

"A"

ABIDE

Abide by: follow a set of rules.

e.g. We must **abide by** all the instructions from the Mayor.

Abide with: stay with someone.

e.g. She is your wife; you must **abide with** her no matter what.

ACCOMMODATE

Accommodate to: adapt to.

e.g. I have to **accommodate** myself **to** the new routine.

Accommodate with: provide something special for someone.

e.g. We will **accommodate** you **with** a new car.

ACE

Ace in (to): be lucky to be admitted into (slang).

e.g. My son **aced into** Harvard University.

Ace out of: be lucky to accomplish something.

e.g. I **aced out of** my chemistry exam.

ADMIT

Admit into: allow someone to enter; allow something to be introduced.

e.g. He was not **admitted into** the concert hall because of his drunken behavior.

e.g. The judge **admitted** the new evidence **into** the trial.

Admit to: confess.

e.g. He found it difficult to **admit** his adultery **to** his wife.

ANSWER

Answer for: be responsible for.

e.g. You will have to **answer for** your mistakes.

Answer to: explain or justify for.

e.g. You will have to **answer to** the judge for what you did.

APPEAL

Appeal against: ask a court to cancel something.

e.g. The lawyer **appealed against** the court's decision.

Appeal for: demand as a right.

e.g. I think we should **appeal for** justice.

e.g. They are **appealing for** our help.

Appeal to: attract or please someone.

e.g. The proposal **appealed** to many of us.

e.g. Her personality **appeals to** everybody around her.

e.g. Does this food **appeal** to your taste?

ARGUE

Argue about: dispute or quarrel with someone over.

e.g. They often **argue about** racial injustice over the dinner table.

Argue against: make a case against someone or something.

e.g. The police discovered new evidence that **argued**

against the criminal charge.

Argue back: answer back.

e.g. I wish he would not **argue back** so much.

Argue down: defeat someone in a debate.

e.g. He tries to **argue down** everyone who has opposite views.

Argue for: make a case for someone.

e.g. My lawyer will **argue for** me in court.

Argue into: convince someone to do something.

e.g. I could not **argue** myself **into** helping you in this project.

Argue with: challenge someone or something.

e.g. I won't **argue with** what you do; after all, it is your choice.

ASK

Ask about: find out more about.

e.g. I want to **ask about** my application for that position.

Ask after: ask about the health and wellbeing of someone.

e.g. My in-laws **asked after** you.

Ask around: request information from a number of people.

e.g. I plan to **ask around** to see what people think about the new Mayor.

Ask back: invite someone to come again.

e.g. Because of your rudeness, they will never **ask** you **back**.

Ask for: request for someone or something.

e.g. The policeman is **asking for** you.

Ask of: ask of something from someone.

e.g. I want to **ask** a favor **of** you.

Ask out: invite someone to go out.

e.g. I **asked** her **out** to dinner, but she refused.

Ask over: invite someone to visit.

e.g. I **asked** my neighbor **over** to fix my computer.

"B"

BACK

Back down: retreat from a position in an argument.

e.g. Knowing that he did not have a valid point, he **backed down** from the argument.

Back out: desert; fail to keep a promise.

e.g. You said you would help us, but you **backed out**.

Back out of: fail to keep a promise.

e.g. We cannot **back out of** the contract; we are legally obligated to do what we are supposed to do.

Back up: support.

e.g. Are you going to **back** me **up** if I decide to go ahead with the project?

BLOW

Blow in: visit unexpectedly.

e.g. What a surprise! What **blows** you **in**?

Blow over: end without causing harm.

e.g. The Mayor expected the riot would **blow over** in a day or two.

Blow up: become very angry.

e.g. As soon as he heard the bad news, he **blew up** and started shouting and screaming.

BOIL

Boil down to: come down to the essential.

e.g. It all **boils down to** the question of who is going to win in the election.

BOTTOM

Bottom out: finally reach the lowest point.

e.g. Investors believed that the stock market would soon **bottom out**.

BREAK

Break down: analyze; itemize.

e.g. Can you **break down** the budget?

e.g. Please **break down** the bill so that we know what we were paying for.

Break down: cease to function; become ill.

e.g. My old car **broke down** on the highway.

e.g. When she heard the tragic news, she **broke down** in tears.

Break in: use something new until it is comfortable.

e.g. This is a wild horse; you have to **break** it **in** before riding on it.

e.g. The mechanic is trying to **break in** the new equipment.

Break in: cut in; interrupt.

e.g. It is rude to **break in** while someone is talking.

Break off: end; stop abruptly.

e.g. He announced that he had **broken off** his engagement.

e.g. In the middle of his speech, he **broke off**, and left the hall.

Break out: arise suddenly or violently.

e.g. A riot **broke out** last night, and many shops were robbed and vandalized.

Break up: stop a relationship; disperse.

e.g. They **broke up** after a twenty-year marriage.

e.g. The police used tear gas to **break up** the crowd demonstrating in front of the City Hall.

BRING

Bring about: cause something to happen.

e.g. The racial discrimination **brought about** the social unrest.

e.g. The sex scandal **brought about** the resignation of the Senator.

Bring off: achieve something difficult.

e.g. The research on DNA was difficult and unpredictable, but the scientists were able to **bring** it **off**.

Bring on: cause something to happen.

e.g. What **brought** the event **on**?

e.g. The riot was **brought on** by the Mayor's proposed policy.

Bring to: revive; make it clear.

e.g. The man fainted, but was soon **brought to** with some smelling salt.

e.g. I hope this incident will **bring** you **to** your senses.

Bring to a close: end something.

e.g. I hope this verdict will finally **bring** the matter **to a close**.

Bring out: emphasize.

e.g. That tragedy **brought out** the best of humanity: all the neighbors were caring and compassionate.

Bring up: raise; care for.

e.g. In this day and age, it is not easy to **bring up** children.

BRUSH

Brush off: dismiss or reject as unimportant or irrelevant.

e.g. The reporter wanted to see the President, but he was **brushed off**.

e.g. This might be a serious problem. Don't just **brush** it **off**!

Brush up: improve.

e.g. It's time you **brushed up** your English.

"C"

CALL

Call for: require.

e.g. This job **calls for** much hard work and responsibility. Do you have what it takes?

Call off: cancel.

e.g. Due to the bad weather, the meeting was **called off**.

Call on: visit; appeal for help.

e.g. I'll **call on** you some time next week.

e.g. We may have to **call on** members for extra donation.

Call up: telephone.

e.g. Don't **call** me **up** unless it is something urgent.

CANCEL

Cancel out: kill; eliminate (slang).

e.g. He hated her so much that he wished he could **cancel** her **out**.

CATCH

Catch on: understand.

e.g. The technology is fairly simple; before long, you'll **catch on**.

Catch up with: keep pace with.

e.g. Hurry up! You have to **catch up with** them; they're well ahead of you.

CHECK

Check out: leave; pay bills.

e.g. We are going to **check out** the hotel at noon.

e.g. I think we have enough money to **check out**.

Check up on: investigate.

e.g. The accountant will **check up on** the sum of money unaccounted for.

CHOP

Chop down: cut down.

e.g. We have to **chop down** some of the trees in the backyard.

Chop up: cut into small pieces.

e.g. You need to **chop up** the onion first.

CLEAR

Clear of: show someone is innocent.

e.g. After the investigation, the police **cleared** me **of** all charges.

Clear off: depart.

e.g. As soon as the police arrived, the crowd began to **clear off**.

Clear out: get out of some place.

e.g. The fire alarm is on; everybody has to **clear out**!

Clear up: clarify something; improve.

e.g. Can you **clear up** this statement for me?

e.g. His cold **cleared up** after a week.

e.g. The sky finally **cleared up**, and we could see the sun.

Clear with: get the approval of.

e.g. We will have to **clear** this **with** the Mayor's office.

CLOCK

Clock out: record time of departure.

e.g. All employees are required to **clock out** at the end of the day.

Clock up: reach a goal.

e.g. He had many goals in life, and he had **clocked up** many of them.

CLOSE

Close down: close permanently; out of business.

e.g. The factory **closed down** last month due to the bad

economy.

Close in: encircle and threaten.

e.g. We are now **closing in** on our enemies.

Close up: close temporarily.

e.g. Come back tomorrow; we're now **closing up**.

CUT

Cut back: reduce the use or the amount of something.

e.g. We should **cut back** on our grocery spending every month.

Cut down: destroy someone's argument; reduce the price of something.

e.g. The lawyer quickly **cut down** his testimony.

e.g. The owner decided to **cut down** his asking price for this house.

Cut in: interrupt.

e.g. Don't **cut in** when someone is talking; it's very rude.

Cut off: turn off of a road.

e.g. This is where you are supposed to **cut off** and make a right turn.

Cut out to be: destined to be.

e.g. He was **cut out to be** a scientist: he had amazing power of exploring and reasoning.

Cut something out: stop doing something.

e.g. **Cut** that **out**! Stop making that noise!

Cut to the quick: hurt someone badly (figuratively).

e.g. His remark **cut** his wife **to the quick**, and she immediately left the room.

"D"

DALLY

Dally over: waste time doing something.

e.g. Don't **dally over** your food. Just eat it!

Dally with: flirt with someone.

e.g. Don't **dally with** that girl; she has no interest in you.

DANCE

Dance on air: be very happy.

e.g. When she heard the good news, she was **dancing on air**.

Dance to another tune: change one's manner, act very differently.

e.g. What I'm going to tell you will make you **dance to another tune**. Be prepared!

DELIGHT

Delight in: take great pleasure in.

e.g. We all **delight in** your baby.

Delight with: please someone with something.

e.g. He **delighted** his wife **with** a diamond bracelet.

DELIVER

Deliver from: save or rescue from.

e.g. The man stranded on the roof was finally **delivered from** danger.

Deliver of: free from burden or problem.

e.g. What a relief now that we are **delivered of** our debt.

Deliver up: yield something to someone.

e.g. Will you **deliver up** the documents to the judge?

DETAIL

Detail for: choose someone to do a particular job.

e.g. I was **detailed for** welcoming all the guests.

DETER

Deter from: prevent or stop.

e.g. I can't **deter** my son **from** drinking alcohol.

e.g. It is not easy to **deter** teenagers **from** their foolish ways.

DIE

Die away: disappear.

e.g. The noise **died away** and it was silent.

Die down: diminish.

e.g. The music has **died down** after midnight.

Die out: disappear gradually.

e.g. This ancient custom is slowly **dying out**.

DIFFER

Differ about: disagree about.

e.g. We **differ about** who should be the next president.

Differ from: be different from.

e.g. How does this one **differ from** that one?

Differ in: be different in a specific way.

e.g. This one and that one **differ in** color.

Differ with: disagree with.

e.g. I **differ with** you on many issues.

DIG

Dig one's heels in: become very stubborn.

e.g. It's useless to talk to her; she has already **dug her heels in**.

Dig in: begin to eat (slang).

e.g. The children are all ready to **dig in** to the birthday cake.

Dig up: find out some gossip about.

e.g. The campaign is eager to **dig up** some dirt on the opponent.

Dig up: locate someone or something (colloquial).

e.g. I'm sure I can **dig up** a date for the meeting.

e.g. Can you **dig up** a substitute when I'm on my maternity leave?

DINE

Dine at: eat at a place.

e.g. We love to **dine at** that fancy restaurant.

Dine in: eat at home.

e.g. I prefer to **dine in** tonight.

Dine off: make a meal out of something.

e.g. We could **dine off** the fish we caught today.

Dine out: eat away from home.

e.g. Maybe we should **dine out** this weekend.

DRESS

Dress down: scold severely.

e.g. The manager **dressed** him **down** right in front of all the employees.

Dress up: put clothes on; adorn.

e.g. Wow! Look at you! You really get **dressed up** for the party in this fancy dress!

DRIFT

Drift apart: separate slowly.

e.g. He **drifted apart** from his friends and lived a secluded life.

Drift back: go back to someone or something slowly.

e.g. He **drifted back** to her former girlfriend, and they were soon married.

Drift off: move away slowly.

e.g. The boat **drifted off** and it disappeared in the thick fog.

Drift off to sleep: fall asleep gradually.

e.g. He sat on the sofa, and finally **drifted off to sleep**.

DRINK

Drink down: consume something by drinking it.

e.g. He **drank down** the medicine, and felt better.

Drink in: absorb sight or information.

e.g. He was standing on the beach, trying to **drink in** the beauty around.

e.g. It would take time to **drink in** the significance of the message.

Drink under the table: be able to drink more alcohol that someone else.

e.g. I bet I can **drink** you **under the table**.

Drink up: consume all of something.

e.g. Do you think you can **drink up** this bottle of wine?

DROP

Drop around: come for a casual visit.

e.g. You must **drop around** some time and have a drink with us.

Drop behind: fail to keep up with a schedule.

e.g. I **dropped behind** in my work because of my ill health recently.

Drop by: visit.

e.g. I hope you can **drop by** and see our new granddaughter.

Drop it on: give some bad news.

e.g. I'm sorry I've to **drop** some bad news **on** you.

"E"

EASE

Ease of: relieve or reduce someone of something.

e.g. The doctor **eased** me **of** my back pain with some medication.

Ease off: diminish; let up doing something.

e.g. The rain has **eased off**; we'd better leave now.

e.g. Come on, he's just a kid. **Ease off**!

Ease up on: treat gently.

e.g. Come on! **Ease up on** the gas! We're going too fast!

EAT

Eat up: consume too much (figuratively).

e.g. This big project has **eaten** me **up**.

EGG

Egg on: encourage someone to do something.

e.g. She is determined to do that. You don't need to **egg** her **on**.

EKE

Eke out: increase or extend.

e.g. He is doing two jobs to **eke out** his income.

EMBARK

Embark for: leave for a place.

e.g. We'll **embark for** Vancouver next month.

Embark on: begin a journey.

e.g. This is the right way to **embark on** your career.

EMBEZZLE

Embezzle from: steal from.

e.g. He had **embezzled** large funds **from** the company, and was now arrested.

END

End up at: be at some place or something at the end.

e.g. The plane **ended up** at Cleveland because of the storm.

End up doing: have to do something unwillingly.

e.g. She didn't want to do that, but **she ended up doing** it anyway.

End up somehow: come to the end of something in a particular way.

e.g. Nobody would like to **end up this way**: losing your home in a tornado.

End up something: become something at the end of everything.

e.g. I never knew I would **end up being** a lawyer instead of a doctor.

ENSUE

Ensue from: result from.

e.g. The riot **ensued from** the proposed policies of the Mayor.

ENTICE

Entice away: lure away or distract from.

e.g. We could not **entice** him **away** from the football game.

e.g. Food **enticed** the children **away** from the television.

EXPEND

Expend on: use something on.

e.g. You **expended** too much energy **on** doing this, and you now look exhausted.

"F"

FACE

Face into: turn something or someone towards a certain direction.

e.g. Please **face into** the camera; they want to take a picture of you.

Face off: prepare for a confrontation.

e.g. The two candidates are going to **face off** in a national debate.

Face up: confront something with courage.

e.g. This is a huge challenge that you must **face up**.

FADE

Fade down: diminish.

e.g. The thunder **faded down**, and soon the sun came out.

Fade up: increase the sound gradually.

e.g. Let's **fade up** the music when the speaker finished his speech.

FALL

Fall apart: break into pieces.

e.g. This old house is **falling apart**; we'd better sell it as soon as possible.

e.g. After the death of his wife, his life began to **fall apart**.

Fall away: drop away from something.

e.g. The paint is **falling away** from the side of the house.

Fall back on: use someone or something as reserve.

e.g. Your father is someone you can **fall back on** when you run out of money.

e.g. We **fell back on** the emergency generator when the power went out.

Fall behind: lag behind schedule.

e.g. You are **falling behind** in your mortgage payments.

e.g. Get cracking, and don't **fall behind** your work.

Fall by: drop in value.

e.g. The gold price **fell by** 10 percent within this week.

Fall down on the job: fail to do a job efficiently.

e.g. If you keep **falling down on the job**, you will be fired!

Fall for: be in love with someone.

e.g. He had **fallen for** his cousin, and soon they became engaged.

Fall in with: become involved with someone or something.

e.g. I am afraid he has **fallen in with** the wrong group with people.

e.g. Your son has **fallen in with** drugs and alcohol.

Fall into disfavor: lose one's influence.

e.g. The Mayor has **fallen into disfavor** with his supporters; he might lose in the coming re-election.

Fall into disgrace: become without honor.

e.g. The Governor **fell into disgrace** because of his involvement with the murder case.

Fall into disuse: be used less and less.

e.g. Your car has **fallen into disuse**; if I were you, I would sell it.

FIND

Find out: discover; learn.

e.g. The police eventually **found out** the truth of the murder case.

e.g. Sooner or later you will **find out** all the facts.

FOLLOW

Follow on: die at a date later than someone.

e.g. His wife passed away. He **followed on** a few months later.

Follow through: continue to supervise.

e.g. I hope someone would **follow through** on this project until its completion.

Follow up: check something out.

e.g. Please **follow up** this lead, and see what will happen next.

FORK

Fork out: pay (slang).

e.g. To go on this trip, you need to **fork out** $2,000.

Fork up: serve something with a fork.

e.g. Could you **fork up** another piece of chicken?

FROWN

Frown at: scowl at someone or something.

e.g. She **frowned at** my cat and gave her a kick.

Frown on: show disapproval.

e.g. His parents **frown on** everything he does.

FUSS

Fuss about: complain about this and that.

e.g. Don't **fuss about** this and that! Everything will be fine!

Fuss over: go to a lot of bother about.

e.g. Don't **fuss over** your hair!

Fuss with: keep bothering.

e.g. Don't **fuss with** your children; they're young adults now!

"G"

GAIN

Gain in: advance in something.

e.g. As you age, you may **gain in** wisdom.

Gain on: begin to catch up with.

e.g. We were able to **gain on** the car in front of us.

Gain dominion over: achieve authority or control over.

e.g. We were able to **gain dominion over** our enemies.

GASP

Gasp at: inhale sharply in surprise.

e.g. The audience **gasped at** what the candidate was saying about the President.

Gasp for air: fight for a breath of air.

e.g. The small room was so crowded that everybody was **gasping for** air.

GET

Get across: cause something to be understood.

e.g. It took the manager some time before he could **get across** the company's new policies to his employees.

Get ahead: advance.

e.g. If you wish to **get ahead** in your career, you must have a higher degree.

Get ahead of: surpass; beat.

e.g. Beware of your assistant; he is an ambitions man who may want to **get ahead of** you.

Get along / get along with: have a good relationship.

e.g. The two of you seem to **get along** quite well.

e.g. Do you think you can **get along with** your in-laws?

Get around: avoid; circulate.

e. g. Is there a way to **get around** this problem, instead of solving it?

e.g. The gossip has been **getting around** that you will soon be married.

Get away: escape.

e.g. The burglar **got away** before the police arrived.

Get away with murder: do something wrong without being punished (usually figuratively).

e.g. Do you think you can really **get away with murder** this time?

Get by: manage somehow.

e.g. I can **get by** with only one part-time job.

Get down to: be serious about.

e.g. Let's **get down to** work!

e.g. You should **get down to** solving the problem, instead of avoiding it.

Get a grip on: control oneself;. get a good understanding of.

e.g. Calm down! **Get a grip on** yourself!

e.g. **Get a grip on** the situation before you make any decision.

Get in: enter.

e.g. Please **get in** the car; we are leaving right now.

Get in on the ground floor: join something in its beginning.

e.g. If you are starting a new project, I would surely like to **get in on the ground floor**.

Get it in the neck: receive trouble or punishment.

e.g. If you don't listen to my advice, you will **get it in the neck**.

Get off it: stop acting so arrogantly.

e.g. **Get off it**! Stop your bully!

Get someone off: clear someone of a criminal charge.

e.g. His lawyer was unable to **get** him **off**, and he was convicted.

Get on: put on.

e.g. It's raining; **get on** your raincoat.

Get on in years: grow older.

e.g. When you **get on in years**, you might think quite differently.

Get on with: continue or proceed with an activity.

e.g. **Get on with** your work; you have to finish it before you leave.

Get over: recover from.

e.g. I got the flu last week, but now I'm **getting over** it.

e.g. The country was **getting over** the economic downturn.

Get a rise out of someone: make someone angry.

e.g. His derogatory remark did **get a rise out of** the audience.

Get the hang of: learn how something is done.

e.g. If you follow the instructions, you will **get the hang of** operating the machine.

Get through: end or finish.

e.g. We were having some financial problems, but now we're **getting through**.

Get up: rise out of bed.

e.g. **Get up**! You'll be late for work!

GIVE

Give in: cave in; give way to; yield to, or give up to someone or something.

e.g. When we kicked the wall, it **gave in**.

e.g. You should not have **given in** to his demand.

e.g. She always **gives in** when under emotional stress or pressure from her parents.

Give rise to: cause something to happen.

e.g. His inflammatory speech **gave rise to** social unrest.

Give a leg up: give someone a helping hand.

e.g. Please **give** her **a leg up**; she needs your moral support.

Give way to: yield to someone or something.

e.g. The cars **gave way to** the pedestrians.

e.g. The Mayor **gave way to** the demands of his supporters.

GLOAT

Gloat over: be glad that something unfortunate has happened to someone else.

e.g. You should not **gloat over** the divorce of your ex-girlfriend.

GLOSS

Gloss over: cover up or minimize the effect of something.

e.g. Don't try to **gloss over** the financial impact of the failure of this project.

e.g. You cannot **gloss over** the pivotal role you had played in these matters.

GO

Go above and beyond one's duty: exceed what is expected or required of one.

e.g. Do you know that doing what you ask **goes above and beyond my duty**?

Go against the grain: run counter to one's ideas or principles.

e.g. Taking this without permission **goes against the grain**.

e.g. It **goes against the grain** not to lift a finger to help a close member of your family who is in dire need of your help.

Go astray: get lost.

e.g. My keys have **gone astray** again! Please help me look for them!

Go back on: reverse one's position.

e.g. I really don't want to **go back on** my word, but an emergency has happened.

Go for broke: risk everything.

e.g. She **went for broke** and decided to marry him despite all the rumors about his infidelity.

Go for nothing: fail to achieve anything.

e.g. All our efforts helping out **went for nothing**.

Go in for: enjoy doing something.

e.g. I don't **go in for** that kind of sport.

Go off the deep end: overdo something.

e.g. You have the habit of **going off the deep end** about almost everything.

Go out of one's head: go crazy.

e.g. He saw what happened in front of his eyes, and **went out of his head**.

Go to pot: degrade or decline in value.

e.g. Our neighborhood has **gone to pot** in the last couple of years.

Go to seed: decline in looks due to neglect.

e.g. Our house has **gone to seed** due to years of neglect.

Go to the dogs: go to ruin; fail completely.

e.g. The election has **gone to the dogs** due to lack of funding.

Go under: fail.

e.g. We tried to keep the project from **going under**, but we did not succeed.

Go up in the world: advance with fame and fortune.

e.g. He was one of the very few young men who could **go up in the world** in so short a time.

GOUGE

Gouge out: cheat someone out of something.

e.g. Don't try to **gouge** some money **out** of that poor old man.

GROUND

Ground in: instruct.

e.g. We should **ground** our children **in** love and values as they grow up.

Ground on: form a foundation for.

e.g. His intelligence was **grounded on** reading books on wisdom.

"H"

HAND

Hand down: deliver; leave as an inheritance.

e.g. We have **handed down** all the information to our associates.

e.g. When he dies, he will **hand down** his business to his family, and not before.

Hand in: submit.

e.g. I have **handed in** my resignation; tomorrow will be my last day in the office.

Hand over: yield control of.

e.g. The manager has **handed over** the human resources section to the assistant manager.

HANG

Hang around: loiter some place and do nothing.

e.g. Stop **hanging around**! Find something to do!

Hang back: lag behind.

e.g. Come on, get moving! Don't **hang back**!

Hang by a thread: barely continue.

e.g. The woman's life **hung by a thread** while she desperately waited for someone to rescue her from the fire that was consuming her house.

Hang in the balance: wait for something to happen to cause a decision to be made.

e.g. The decision whether to have the surgery or not will **hang in the balance** until the medical report comes back.

Hang on: wait awhile.

e.g. **Hang on**. I'll catch up with you.

Hang on someone's every word: listen carefully.

e.g. I am **hanging on** your **every word**. Please give me some detailed instructions.

Hang something on someone: blame someone for something.

e.g. Don't try to **hang** the blame **on** your wife; it was you who made the decision.

Hang out: spend time in a place.

e.g. Where are you going to **hang out** with your friends this evening?

Hang over: worry about something.

e.g. I have the credit card debt **hanging over** me. I don't know how to pay back.

HAVE

Have a thing about: have a fear of or dislike about.

e.g. I **have a thing about** public speaking; it's never my cup of tea.

Have one's wits about one: be alert.

e.g. You'd better **have** your **wits about** you when you go to see the attorney.

Have someone around: invite someone to visit.

e.g. Next time, I'll **have** your cousins **around** for an evening of bridge.

Have back at: get even with someone.

e.g. I am going to **have back at** you for talking behind my back.

Have a crush on: have intense love for.

e.g. I think your daughter **has a crush on** that handsome young man.

Have a flair for: have the talent for something.

e.g. She **has a flair for** making fancy dresses.

Have a leg up on: have an advantage over someone.

e.g. He **has a leg up on** his brother when it comes to dealing with strangers.

Have a nose for: have the ability to sense or find something.

e.g. Your wife **has a nose for** gossip.

Have a score to settle with: have a disagreement to resolve with someone.

e.g. I **have a score to settle with** you over this legal issue.

Have a stake in: have something at risk.

e.g. I don't **have a stake in** the stock market; I don't care if it is going to plunge.

Have it out with: argue or settle someone with something.

e.g. I have been at odds with him for a while. Now, I'm going to **have it out with** him once and for all.

HEAD

Head off: intercept or divert someone or something.

e.g. I think we can **head off** the problem this time.

e.g. Don't worry. We can **head** it **off** with another new project

Head out: begin a journey.

e.g. What time do we **head out** tomorrow morning?

Head up: be in charge of something.

e.g. I think I shall **head up** the committee soon.

HELP

Help along: help someone move along.

e.g. We are more than happy to **help** you **along** by giving you any assistance.

Help on with: help someone to put on something.

e.g. Please **help** her **on with** her coat.

Help out: help someone out at a particular place.

e.g. I'm at the kitchen. Can you **help** me **out**?

Help someone to something: serve something to someone.

e.g. **Help** yourself **to** more rice pudding.

HIT

Hit below the belt: treat unfairly.

e.g. Stop that! You're **hitting** me **below the belt**! It's totally unfair!

Hit between the eyes: strike someone suddenly and hard.

e.g. His marriage to that woman **hit** me **between the eyes**. It was beyond my comprehension.

Hit on: discover.

e.g. The man **hit on** the secret love affair of his wife when he was looking through her drawers.

Hit up for something: ask someone for a loan or special favor.

e.g. My son **hit** me **up for** a few hundred dollars.

Hit it off with: have a good relationship with.

e.g. You really **hit it off with** your new boss.

HOLD

Hold at bay: keep someone or something at a safe distance.

e.g. The bombing might be able to **hold** the enemies **at bay**, at least for a while.

e.g. The man could no longer **hold** his anger **at bay**, and he took out his gun and pointed at the policeman.

Hold back on: withhold something.

e.g. **Hold back on** this. We might need it in the days to come.

Hold by: stick to a promise.

e.g. I hope you will **hold by** this agreement.

Hold good for: remain open, such as an offer to someone or something.

e.g. Does it still **hold good for** everyone here, including members of the family?

Hold no brief for: not to tolerate someone or something.

e.g. We should **hold no brief for** social injustice.

Hold off: delay or postpone doing something.

e.g. Can you **hold off** buying this new car? We can't afford it.

Hold out: survive.

e.g. I don't think we can **hold out** much longer with this kind of income.

Hold a candle to: be equal to someone or something.

e.g. You don't **hold a candle to** your brother when it comes to playing the guitar.

Hold one's head up: be confident.

e.g. **Hold** your **head up** when it comes to public speaking.

Hold still for: put up with something.

e.g. It is not easy to **hold still for** that kind of rude remark.

Hold up on: delay or postpone further action.

e.g. **Hold up on** the appointment; we may have a better candidate.

Hold with: agree or tolerate something.

e.g. I don't think I can **hold with** your preposition.

HOODWINK

Hoodwink into: deceive someone into doing something.

e.g. Don't try to **hoodwink** me **into** doing this for you for free.

Hoodwink someone out of: get something away by deception.

e.g. Don't try to **hoodwink** me **out of** my money!

HOPE

Hope against hope: hope when something is almost hopeless.

e.g. You're **hoping against hope** that he will ever come back to you.

Hope for: be optimistic about.

e.g. We should **hope for** a better future.

Hope for the best: desire the best to come.

e.g. Good luck! We all **hope for the best**.

HOLD

Hold no brief for: tolerate someone or something.

e.g. I **hold no brief for** that kind of bad behavior.

Hold off: delay; restrain.

e.g. We can no longer **hold off** the launching of the sales campaign

e.g. The air strike might somehow **hold off** the enemies for some time.

Hold one's end up: carry one's share of the bargain or burden.

e.g. We expect you to **hold** your **end up** and keep your promise to back us up.

Hold out: survive.

e.g. With only this much money, I don't know how long we could **hold out**.

HORSE

Horse around: play around nosily and roughly.

e.g. Don't **horse around**! It's time to go home!

HOVER

Hover around: hang or wait around.

e.g. The birds **hovered around** the bird feeder.

Hover between: waver in choosing between this and that.

e.g. You should not **hover between** these two options. Just make up your mind!

HUNGER

Hunger after: crave for.

e.g. The child **hungered after** a dessert.

Hunger for: desire (figuratively).

e.g. He is really madly in love and **hungers for** you.

e.g. My son **hungers for** success in the real estate.

"I"

IDENTIFY

Identify as: determine someone as.

e.g. He was **identified as** the killer.

Identify by: recognize someone or something as.

e.g. I can **identify** my baggage **by** that special mark.

Identify with: associate or classify with.

e.g. Do you **identify** yourself **with** that group of teenagers?

e.g. People usually **identify** green **with** grass.

IMMERSE

Immerse in: give a lot of information or instruction to.

e.g. The man **immersed** himself **in** his studies before the bar exam.

e.g. The new instructor **immersed** the whole class **in** the fundamentals of engineering.

IMPART

Impart to: tell something to someone.

e.g. The speaker **imparted** great wisdom **to** the audience.

e.g. I wish I could **impart** my knowledge **to** you.

e.g. She wanted to **impart** an air of elegance **to** her presence.

IMPRESS

Impress as: be memorable to someone as.

e.g. She **impressed** the audience **as** an accomplished pianist.

Impress by: make someone notice one's good quality.

e.g. She **impressed** me **by** her honesty and sincerity.

Impress into: press something into something.

e.g. The child **impressed** his finger **into** the birthday cake.

Impress with: awe someone with someone or something.

e.g. Are you trying to **impress** me **with** your beautiful girlfriend?

e.g. You **impressed** the audience **with** your profound wisdom.

INCH

Inch across: creep slowly across.

e.g. The injured dog **inched across** the bridge.

Inch back: go back slowly.

e.g. The army **inched back** as we fired our guns.

Inch over: move back a little.

e.g. Can you **inch over** a little? I can't get in.

INCLINE

Incline away from: lean away from.

e.g. I had to **incline away from** him because he strongly smelled of tobacco.

Incline forward: lean forward.

e.g. Please **incline forward** so that you can see better from here.

Incline toward: favor or have a preference for.

e.g. I **incline toward** choosing medical science as my career.

INCLUDE

Include among: choose or classify.

e.g. He **included** himself **among** the top writers of science fiction.

Include in: invite.

e.g. I think we'll **include** him **in** the party.

INFORM

Inform about: tell someone about someone or something.

e.g. I will **inform** you **about** your son's academic progress from time to time.

Inform of: provide facts about.

e.g. The lawyer will **inform** us **of** the decision of the court.

Inform on: tell the authorities of someone or something.

e.g. We must **inform** the police **on** the disappearance of the documents.

e.g. I think he was the guy who **informed on** you.

INFUSE

Infuse into: put some knowledge into someone's brain.

e.g. I was able to **infuse** all the instructions **to** the new employees.

Infuse with: provide knowledge.

e.g. Children should be **infused with** honesty and integrity at any early age.

INQUIRE

Inquire about: ask about.

e.g. We can **inquire about** that at the front desk.

Inquire after: ask about the well-being of someone.

e.g. He **inquired after** her in-laws when he saw her this morning.

Inquire for: ask to see someone.

e.g. He was the guy who **inquired for** you, but I told him that you were busy.

Inquire into: investigate.

e.g. The police would **inquire into** your complaint.

Inquire of: ask information of someone.

e.g. I'm afraid we have to **inquire** you **of** your income tax.

INSTILL

Instill into: impress someone with something.

e.g. The teacher is trying to **instill** good behavior **into** her pupils.

Instill with: teach or indoctrinate something to someone.

e.g. The speaker **instilled** the audience **with** self-confidence and positive thinking.

INTEND

Intend as: mean something to serve as something.

e.g. I **intend** this money **as** the college fund for your grandchild.

Intend for: mean for someone or something to get something.

e.g. Your mother **intended** this cake **for** your party with your friends.

e.g. I **intended** this one specially **for** you, and no one else.

INTERVENE

Intervene between: intercede between.

e.g. My two brothers were arguing so fiercely that I had to **intervene between** them.

Intervene in: get involved.

e.g. The manager had to **intervene in** the growing racial discrimination in his office.

INTIMIDATE

Intimidate into: threaten someone into doing something.

e.g. You cannot **intimidate** me **into** doing this for you.

Intimidate with: threaten someone with something.

e.g. Do you think you can **intimidate** me **with** your bully?

"J"

JACK

Jack around: waste time (slang).

e.g. Don't **jack around**! Find something to do!

Jack someone around: give someone a difficult time (slang).

e.g. Please don't **jack** me **around**!

Jack up: increase or stimulate (slang).

e.g. Pharmaceutical companies have **jacked up** the prices of their drugs.

e.g. I tried to **jack** him **up** with encouragement.

e.g. She **jacked** herself **up** with a dose of alcohol.

JAM

Jam into: force someone or something into.

e.g. Don't try to **jam** us all **into** that small room.

e.g. He **jammed** all his clothes **into** that bag.

Jam on: press down hard on.

e.g. Don't **jam on** your brake! Be easy on it!

JOCKEY

Jockey around: move around to get into a special position.

e.g. Many drivers have to **jockey around** when they get into a parking place.

Jockey for: work into a desired position.

e.g. Many candidates **jockeyed for** that position but without any success.

JOIN

Join forces with: combine efforts with.

e.g. If you **join forces with** us, we can accomplish this project.

JUICE

Juice back: drink all of it (slang).

e.g. He **juiced back** the whole glass of beer.

Juice up: make something more powerful, or get more alcohol (slang).

e.g. It's too dark; can we **juice up** the light?

e.g. Don't spend more money to **juice up** your car.

e.g. Let's go out tonight, and **juice up** at that bar.

JUMP

Jump all over: scold.

e.g. What's wrong with you? You're **jumping all over** me! I'd nothing to do with that!

Jump out of one's skin: be very shocked.

e.g. She was so frightened that she almost **jumped out of her skin**.

Jump through hoops: do what one is told to do.

e.g. The manager expects all his staff to **jump through hoops**.

Jump to conclusion: come to conclusion too quickly.

e.g. Please look at the facts first, and don't **jump to conclusion**.

"K"

KEEP

Keep one's wits about one: be alert.

e.g. In this neighborhood, you should always **keep your wits about you** at all times.

Keep your head above water: survive, especially

financially.

e.g. Taking good care of your finance will **keep your head above water**.

Keep ahead of: remain in advance of someone or something.

e.g. She is so talented and knowledgeable in this field that it is difficult for me to **keep ahead of** her.

e.g. I **kept ahead of** him throughout the race.

Keep apart: separate them.

e.g. I don't know how to **keep** your cat and your dog **apart**.

Keep at: continue to do something.

e.g. You must **keep at** it until it is done.

e.g. To succeed, you have to **keep at** this.

Keep at bay: hold off someone or something.

e.g. Our fierce dog can **keep** all intruders **at bay**.

Keep down: prevent someone or something from advancing.

e.g. This might **keep down** the oil price for a while.

e.g. Not having a degree will **keep** you **down** in your career advancement.

Keep in good with: remain in favor with.

e.g. You should always **keep in good with** your boss.

Keep in touch with: remain in communication with.

e.g. Even though your children are married, you should always **keep in touch with** them.

Keep in stitches: make someone laughing.

e.g. The comedian was able to **keep** the audience **in stitches**.

Keep in the dark: keep someone ignorant about something.

e.g. You have **kept** me **in the dark** all these years: I didn't know you were already married.

Keep off someone's back: stop criticizing.

e.g. **Keep off my back** and leave me alone!

Keep on at: continue to criticize.

e.g. The senators **kept on at** the healthcare issues.

Keep on: pay close attention to.

e.g. **Keep on** this problem until it is resolved.

Keep one's feet on the ground: be calm and stable.

e.g. Despite the shooting, the speaker was able to **keep his feet on the ground**.

Keep one's nose to the grindstone: work very hard.

e.g. For decades, my father had **kept his nose to the grindstone**, but now he is retired.

Keep to oneself: keep it as a secret.

e.g. I knew about that a long time ago, but I have **kept it to myself**.

Keep to the straight and narrow: stay out of trouble.

e.g. Be a good kid and **keep to the straight and narrow**.

Keep body and soul together: survive without a lot of money.

e.g. "How're you doing?" "Just hanging in there, **keeping body and soul together**."

Keep up with the Joneses: try to have an extravagant lifestyle as one's neighbors.

e.g. We'd better move out of this neighborhood: we just can't **keep up with the Joneses**.

Keep faith with: be loyal to.

e.g. We've pledged to **keep faith with** one another and what we stand for.

KICK

Kick some ass around: show who is in charge (slang).

e.g. The candidate spoke to his supporters and **kicked some ass around**.

Kick back: relax, or return to an addiction (slang).

e.g. It has been a stressful day. I just want to **kick back** and have a cup of hot tea.

e.g. He stopped smoking only for a few days, and then **kicked back**.

Kick in: contribute to something (slang).

e.g. We want to buy her a present. Would you like to **kick in** a few bucks?

Kick over the traces: do what one is not meant to do.

e.g. Today many young kids just want to **kick over the traces**, such as taking drugs.

Kick up a fuss: complain about something insignificant.

e.g. It's serious! I'm not just **kicking up a fuss**!

e.g. Don't **kick up a fuss** about me or what I did!

Kick up one's heels: celebrate and have a good time.

e.g. Today is our anniversary; let's go out tonight, and **kick up our heels**.

KISS

Kiss off: kill (slang).

e.g. The man **kissed off** his rival with a gun.

KNOCK

Knock one's head against a brick wall: become very frustrated.

e.g. Throughout his career, he had **knocked his head against a brick wall** several times.

Knock back a drink: consume a drink.

e.g. She decided to **knock back** a brandy in front of her parents.

Knock it off: shut up!

e.g. Will you **knock it off**? I'm on the phone.

Knock off: stop working; finish something quickly.

e.g. I **knock off** work at seven every day.

e.g. I **knocked** two books **off** within an hour.

Knock out: do something with great effort and energy.

e.g. I **knocked** myself **out** to do this project for you.

Knock over: steal (slang).

e.g. Those teenagers **knocked over** five bottles of beer from that store.

Knock someone over: surprise or shock.

e.g. His abominable behavior **knocked** everyone **over**.

Knock one's knees together: be very frightened.

e.g. I **knocked** my **knees together** when I had to walk through that neighborhood.

KNOW

Know one's way around: know how to get from place to place.

e.g. Don't worry! I won't get lost; I **know my way around**.

Know apart: can tell the differences between.

e.g. Do you **know** these twins **apart**?
able

e.g. The knowledgeable speaker obviously **knows** these two ancient cultures **apart**.

Know by sight: recognize someone's face but not know the name.

e.g. I **know** all my colleagues **by sight** only.

Know one for what one is: recognize one as one type of person one belongs to.

e.g. I **know him for what he is**—a rascal.

Know through and through: know something well.

e.g. The instructor really **knows** his subject **through and through**.

KNUCKLE

Knuckle down: get busy doing something.

e.g. Come on! **Knuckle down**! We don't have much time left.

"L"

LABEL

Label as: designate someone or something as.

e.g. Don't **label** your son **as** dishonest and good for

nothing.

LABOR

Labor for: work on behalf of someone or something.

e.g. I **labored for** you all day long, and you didn't even thank me.

Labor over: work hard on.

e.g. The lawyer **labored over** my case for months.

e.g. The doctor **labored over** his patient for hours.

LAG

Lag behind: fall behind.

e.g. Hurry up, or else we'll **lag behind**.

LAM

Lam into: attack someone or something.

e.g. The angry crowd **lamed into** the policemen.

Land in: cause someone to end up in something.

e.g. The crimes he had committed **landed** him **in** prison.

LAPSE

Lapse from grace: fall into disfavor.

e.g. If you do this without consulting your boss, you will **lapse from grace**.

Lapse into: weaken into something.

e.g. Before the doctor arrived, the injured man **lapsed into** a coma.

LAST

Last for: exist for a period of time.

e.g. The social unrest has **lasted for** some time.

e.g. You'd better come right away; I don't think I can **last for** much longer,

Last out: hold out or tolerate.

e.g. I'd better go now; I can't **last out** listening to his boasting.

LAUGH

Laugh in someone's face: laugh in ridicule.

e.g. It's rude to **laugh in his face**!

Laugh one's head off: laugh hard and loud.

e.g. The comedian was so funny that I almost **laughed** my **head off**.

LAY

Lay at someone's door: put the blame on someone.

Don't **lay** the failure of the project **at** my **door**!

Lay away: bury.

e.g. My father passed away, and we **laid** him **away** last week in a simple ceremony.

Lay down on the job: fail to do it efficiently.

e.g. If you **lay down on the job**, you will be fired!

Lay it on thick: exaggerate something.

e.g. You really know how to **lay it on thick** to flatter and please her.

Lay off: dismiss from employment.

e.g. Many workers were **laid off** during the economic downturn.

Lay one's cards on the table: be candid about one's position.

e.g. Let's **lay** our **cards on the table**, and say exactly what we want to do.

Lay up: make someone ill.

e.g. Many people were **laid up** by the flu.

LEAD

Lead off: be the first one to go.

e.g. You **lead off**, and I'll follow.

Lead astray: mislead or misguide.

e.g. This young man was so naïve that he was **led astray** by his so-called friends.

Lead by the nose: guide someone slowly and carefully.

e.g. His mentor **led** him **by the nose** for many years until he was good and ready.

Lead down the garden path: deceive someone.

e.g. Don't believe what he tells you. He will **lead** you **down the garden path**.

LEAVE

Leave it at that: leave a situation as it is.

e.g. We've done our best. Let's **leave it at that**, and see what happens next.

Leave for: depart for some place.

e.g. We'll **leave for** London tomorrow morning.

Leave up in the air: leave someone waiting for a decision.

e.g. I went to see the Senator for a decision, but was **left up in the air**.

LEND

Lend an ear to: listen to someone.

e.g. **Lend** me your **ear**, and I'll tell you every detail.

Lend itself to: be suitable for something.

e.g. I don't think your dress will **lend itself to** the occasion, which is supposed to be very formal.

LET

Let down: disappointed.

e.g. I put my hope on you; don't **let** me **down**.

Let out: release.

e.g. Don't **let out** your anger on me!

e.g. He was **let out** of prison after he was found not guilty of the crime.

Let up: decrease in intensity.

e.g. After a while, the rain **let up**.

LEVEL

Level against: accuse someone of something.

e.g. The cop is going to **level** an assault charge **against** you.

Level at: direct something at someone.

e.g. The man came out of the crowd and **leveled** insults **at** the Senator.

Level off: decrease in size or amount.

e.g. After a while the supply of the goods will **level off**.

Level with: be honest with someone.

e.g. I'll **level with you**: you will not succeed.

LIE

Lie at death's door: close to dying.

e.g. He was so sick that he **lay at death's door** for a month.

Lie back: relax.

e.g. Just **lie back**! This is not the end of the world!

Lie down on one's job: fail to do one's job.

e.g. If you continue to **lie down on your job**, you will be fired.

Lie in store for: await someone in the future.

e.g. The reality is that we don't know **what lies in store for** us in the days to come

Lie through one's teeth: tell lies shamelessly.

e.g. I know you're **lying in your teeth**! I don't believe a word of what you're saying.

LIGHT

Light a fire under: encourage or excite.

e.g. If you want your son to succeed in that, maybe you should **light a fire under** him.

Light up: become interested.

e.g. When I told her that I made a lot of money during the trip, she immediately **lit up**.

LINGER

Linger on: stay or remain for a long time; live longer than.

e.g. We **lingered on** after most of the guests had left the party.

e.g. My mother **lingered on** several years after my father passed away.

LISTEN

Listen to: pay attention to.

e.g. Please **listen to** what I am going to say.

Listen up: pay attention to and obey (colloquial).

e.g. **Listen up!** You must finish this before you can go.

LIVE

Live beyond one's means: live a lifestyle that one cannot afford.

e.g. If you **live beyond your means**, you will soon go into debt.

Live by one's wits: survive because of one's wisdom or smartness.

e.g. You'll be amazed how he has **lived by his wits** all these years.

Live down: overcome something difficult or embarrassing.

e.g. I don't think I'll ever **live** this humiliation **down**.

e.g. The tragic loss of her children is something she cannot **live down** for the rest of her life.

Live from hand to mouth: live a life of poverty.

e.g. In this day and age, there are many who are **living from hand to mouth**.

Live off: survive by means of.

e.g. You can't **live off** your parents; you need to find a job.

e.g. Somehow he could **live off** his small income.

Live on borrowed time: survive when death is expected any time.

e.g. The doctor told the cancer patient that he was **living on borrowed time**.

LOAF

Loaf around: do nothing.

e.g. You always **loaf around** on your weekends

Loaf away: waste.

e.g. Don't **loaf away** your time and money on this project; it's not worth it.

LONG

Long for: desire or pine for.

e.g. We all **long for** a holiday on these exotic islands.

e.g. A family with loving children is what most married

couples **long for**.

LOOK

Look askance at: be shocked or surprised at.

e.g. Everybody was **looking askance at** the poor performance of the singer.

Look daggers at: look with anger and hatred.

e.g. Don't **look daggers at** me! I didn't take your money!

Look before you leap: be alert before you take any action.

e.g. If I were you, I would **look before I leap**; it may not be as simple as you think.

Look a gift horse in the mouth: be ungrateful or critical of what one receives.

e.g. Don't **look a gift horse in the mouth**! After all, you didn't pay a dime for that!

Look like a million dollars: look very good (colloquial).

e.g. Your new car **looks like a million dollars**!

e.g. You were so depressed the last time I saw you. Wow! Today you **look like a million dollars**!

LOSE

Lose oneself in: be completely absorbed in.

e.g. If you **lose yourself in** your work, time just flies by.

Lose out: lose in competition.

e.g. I **lost out** in the race yesterday, but I did try my best to win.

Lose one's head over: do something foolish.

e.g. Don't **lose your head over** your accomplishment; it may not last.

e.g. Don't **lose your head over** your new girlfriend.

"M"

MAKE

Make an exception for: make a special case for.

e.g. Because of your reputation, they are **making an exception for** you.

e.g. He does not have a higher degree, but they are going to **make an exception for** him due to his well-recognized experience.

Make free with: exploit, or take advantage of.

e.g. You should not **make free with** your secretary: she is not supposed to work for you on weekends.

Make from scratch: start from the basics.

e.g. Without the instructions, we have to **make** it **from scratch**.

Make a habit of: do something so often that it becomes a habit.

e.g. **Make a habit of** saying a prayer before a meal.

Make heads or tails of: understand.

e.g. No one could make **heads or tails of** what he was saying.

Make much of: pay too much attention to.

e.g. I think you do **make much of** what people think of you.

Make nothing of: ignore something bad.

e.g. I was surprised that the Mayor **made nothing of** the riot.

Make of: interpret.

e.g. What do you **make of** the statement of the President?

e.g. Do you want to **make** something **of** it?

Make off with: run away with.

e.g. The bank robber **made off with** $5,000.

Make out: understand with difficulty; write a check.

e.g. It was very difficult to **make out** what he was saying in such a noisy environment.

e.g. He **made out** a check of $20 to his neighbor for helping him.

Make over: remake.

e.g. She **made over** her body: she lost 200 pounds.

e.g. To win in the next election, you need to **make over** the whole team.

Make a pig of oneself: eat too much.

e.g. You've eaten too much already; don't **make a pig of yourself**!

Make points with: impress someone (slang).

e.g. You were just **making points with** your boss; I don't think he was impressed at all.

Make the best of: do as well as possible with something that may not be promising.

e.g. You should **make the best of** this difficult situation.

Make up: invent; apply cosmetics; become reconciled.

e.g. He had to **make up** an excuse explaining why he was so late.

e.g. She **made up** beautifully before she put on the fancy dress.

e.g. After the heated argument, the man and his wife **made up**.

Make up for: compensate.

e.g. We'd better hurry to **make up for** the time lost.

MARK

Mark for life: affect someone for life.

e.g. Her failed marriage is going to **mark** her **for life**.

MARRY

Marry above (below) oneself: marry someone better (or not as good as) oneself.

e.g. She is always thinking of **marrying above herself**—probably a millionaire.

e.g. The professor **married below herself**: her husband did not even finish high school.

Marry one's way out of: get out of something by marrying someone.

e.g. She wants to **marry her way out of** poverty.

MATTER

Matter to: be important to.

e.g. Does it **matter to** you if I don't have a college degree?

MEASURE

Measure up to: compare well to; be what was expected..

e.g. He doesn't **measure up** to his brother in musical talents.

e.g. Your efforts in pursuing music **measure up to** everyone's expectations.

MEET

Meet with: have a meeting with; experience something; encounter a response.

e.g. I **met with** the Senator yesterday.

e.g. The family **met with** a terrible car accident.

e.g. The proposal **met with** much opposition from the public.

MELT

Melt in someone's mouth: be tasty and delicious.

e.g. I hope my potluck dish will **melt in everyone's mouth**.

MESS

Mess around: waste time (colloquial).

e.g. Don't just **mess around**! Can you lend me a hand?

Mess around with: experiment with something to find out more.

e.g. They have been **messing around with** this project to see if it is really beneficial to the public.

Mess over: treat someone badly.

e.g. The woman **messed over** the poor kid until he was finally hospitalized.

Mess up: make untidy; interfere or make it bad.

e.g. She spilled her soup, and **messed up** her beautiful dress.

e.g. His drug addiction **messed up** his life.

MILL

Mill around: wander aimlessly.

e.g. He is **milling around**, looking for something to do.

MOON

Moon away: waste time dreaming for something to happen.

e.g. You have **mooned away** all these years, thinking you would marry a millionaire.

MUDDLE

Muddle along: continue in confusion.

e.g. Without clear instructions, some employees simply **muddled along**.

Muddle around: work inefficiently.

e.g. Many employees were laid off because they were **muddling around**.

"N"

NAIL

Nail someone's ears back: scold severely (slang).

e.g. If you don't do as you were told, she's going to **nail your ears back**.

NOISE

Noise about: gossip.

e.g. Please don't **noise about** my being fired by my boss.

NOSE

Nose about: look here and there for.

e.g. We **nosed about** the streets but couldn't find his whereabouts.

Nose around: pry into something.

e.g. Because she likes to gossip, she is always **nosing around**.

Nose out: defeat someone by a narrow margin.

e.g. In this election, this candidate was **nosed out** by her opponent.

Nut up: go mad (slang).

e.g. If you do this again, I bet she'll **nut up**!

"O"

OBLIGE

Oblige by: accommodate someone by doing something.

e.g. Please **oblige** her **by** going to the party with her.

Oblige to: require someone to do something.

e.g. I **oblige you** to come and pick me up at 8.00 pm tonight.

e.g. You are **obliged to** finish the work before you can leave.

OPT

Opt in: choose to join.

e.g. We **opted in** the club right away.

Opt out: choose not to be in something.

e.g. I **opted out** the new project.

OWN

Own up to: confess or admit

e.g. He **owned up to** his wife that he had misbehaved at the party.

e.g. He finally **owned up to** his infidelity.

"P"

PAD

Pad down: sleep at (slang).

e.g. Can I **pad down** at your place tonight? I've no place to go.

Pad out: make something look larger.

e.g. Can you **pad out** this short report with more information?

PAN

Pan out: turn into success.

e.g. Don't worry; our project will **pan out** all right.

PARTAKE

Partake in: participate in.

e.g. Would you **partake in** the performance? We need someone with your talent.

Partake of: have a portion of.

e.g. Would you like to **partake of** this birthday cake?

PASS

Pass away: die.

e.g. My grandfather **passed away** last Sunday.

Pass for: be accepted as.

e.g. You look just like my brother; you can easily **pass for** him.

Pass out: faint.

e.g. When I heard the bad news, I almost **passed out**.

PAY

Pay off: get good result.

e.g. Your college education will **pay off** in your future career.

Pay through the nose: pay a lot of money.

e.g. The agent knew how to make the customers **pay through the nose**.

PEG

Peg out: die (slang).

e.g. During the police shooting, I thought I was going to **peg out**!

PICK

Pick on: tease; make fun of; bully.

e.g. Don't **pick on** me with you dirty jokes!

e.g. Why do you always **pick on** her when it comes to bullying?

Pick out: select

e.g. You have to **pick out** your favorite songs from this album.

Pick up: lift with hands or fingers; learn; increase quantity or speed.

e.g. Can you **pick up** that piece of paper on the floor?

e.g. You can always **pick up** some colloquial expressions from watching a movie.

e.g. We hope the sales will **pick up** in a few months.

e.g. Our car began to **pick up** speed as soon as it was on the highway.

Pick up the tab: pay the bill.

e.g. Who is going to **pick up the tab** at the restaurant tonight?

PIG

Pig out: eat too much on something, like a pig.

e.g. I decided to **pig out** on ice cream on my birthday.

PILE

Pile up: crash together (cars).

e.g. Yesterday cars **piled up** on this freeway because of the dense fog.

PIN

Pin down: demand a definite answer.

e.g. The reporters tried to **pin** the Senator **down** on more details concerning the event, but they were unsuccessful.

PITCH

Pitch in: join in and help.

e.g. We're going to mow the lawn. Would you like to **pitch in**?

PLACE

Place a strain on: deplete the resources of.

e.g. The demanding job has **placed a strain on** me; I'm thinking of quitting it.

PLAY

Play by ear: play music through hearing.

e.g. The child prodigy **played** his piano **by ear** without taking any lesson.

Play for keeps: do something serious and permanent.

e.g. We're **playing for keeps**, so do your very best.

Play into someone's hands: do exactly as someone wants.

e.g. If you do this, you're **playing into your parents' hands**. Good for you!

Play out: happen or finish.

e.g. After the President's speech, we'll see how things are going to **play out**.

e.g. When the inauguration **plays out**, then everything will return to normal.

Play the devil with: ruin or spoil.

e.g. The stormy weather **played the devil with** my vacation.

Play up: exaggerate someone or something.

e.g. You don't have to **play** him **up**; he will be selected

e.g. You're **playing up** your children's accomplishments.

Play havoc with: mess up someone or something.

e.g. I knew I **played havoc with** you when I said the exact opposite of what you had in mind.

e.g. The manager's proposals **play havoc** with our projects.

POKE

Poke one's nose into: pry into.

e.g. Don't **poke your nose into** my affairs; it's none of your business.

POP

Pop up: appear suddenly.

e.g. Can you guess who **popped up** at my office this morning?

PORE

Pore over: read carefully.

e.g. Please **pore over** all these documents before you make any decision.

PORK

Pork out on: overeat something.

e.g. You mustn't **pork out on** these French fries; just watch your weight!

POUR

Pour it on thick: flatter excessively.

e.g. You really **pour it on thick** just now! I hope you really meant what you said.

Pour oil on troubled waters: calm someone down.

e.g. She was agitated. I hope her Mom could **pour oil over troubled waters**.

Pour one's heart out: express one's personal feelings.

e.g. I'm glad I could **pour** my **heart out** to you.

PULL

Pull the wool over someone's eyes: deceive.

e.g. You can't **pull the wool over his eyes**; he is too smart for you.

Pull through: survive.

e.g. I hope you could **pull through** your cancer treatment.

e.g. Many businesses were able to **pull through** that economic downturn.

Pull oneself together: be calm and sensible.

e.g. **Pull yourself together**, and face the challenge!

PUSH

Push for something: request or demand.

e.g. The Congress is **pushing for** healthcare reforms.

PUT

Put one's foot down: assert something strongly.

e.g. The man finally **put his foot down**, and said, "Take it or leave it!"

Put something down to: say something is caused by something.

e.g. I **put** my success **down to** my perseverance, rather than my good fortune.

Put one's best foot forward: try to make a good impression.

e.g. In the job interview, **put your best foot forward**.

Put in a good word: say something good about.

e.g. If you see my boss, **put in a good word** for me.

Put in for: apply.

e.g. I've **put in for** a transfer to another department.

Put one's foot in one's mouth: say something one shouldn't have said.

e.g. You not only have a loud mouth; but also **put your foot in your mouth**.

Put in a nutshell: summarize it concisely.

e.g. To **put it in a nutshell**: we accomplished the job on time!

Put words in someone's mouth: interpret someone's words according to what one wants and not what the speaker meant.

e.g. Don't **put words in my mouth**: I didn't say that, and I didn't mean that!

Put on airs: pretend to act better.

e.g. Be yourself, and don't **put on airs**!

Put someone on the spot: force someone to make a decision or take an action.

e.g. The reporters **put** the President **on the spot**, and he had to either admit or deny it.

Put oneself out: inconvenience oneself.

e.g. I don't know why I **put myself out** for you; I don't have to drive you home!

"Q"

Queue up: line up.

e.g. We have to **queue up** to get into the concert hall

"R"

RACK

Rack up: damage.

e.g. How did you **rack up** your car like that?

RAG

Rag about: complain to someone about.

e.g. Why do you **rag** me **about** your parents every time I see you?

RAIL

Rail against: complain strongly against.

e.g. The demonstrators **railed against** the decision of the Supreme Court.

Rail at: scold at.

e.g. What's wrong with you? Why are you railing at me for something that I did not do?

RAILROAD

Railroad into: force someone to do something.

e.g. You cannot **railroad** me **into** doing this for you!

RAIN

Rain on someone's parade: spoil or ruin someone's plans (figuratively).

e.g. Why do you always **rain on** your daughter's weekend **parade**?

RAISE

Raise a stink about: make it into an issue or a problem.

e.g. Don't **raise a stink about** everything that happens to you.

Raise hell with: cause serious problems.

e.g. This is going to **raise hell with** your tight schedule next week.

RAKE

Rake in: pull something in.

e.g. Our advertising campaign had **raked in** a lot of sales.

Rake over the coals: chastise or scold.

e.g. The manager **raked** him **over the coals** for being late all the time.

RANK

Rank above: be better or higher than.

e.g. You always think you **rank above** me in everything I do.

Rank among: be included in a particular group.

e.g. He **ranked among** the best pianists.

Rank with: be equal to.

e.g. Do you think I can **rank with** her in playing chess?

RAP

Rap with: have a conversation with.

e.g. Come in, and **rap with** us for a while.

REACH

Reach an understanding with: come to an agreement or

a settlement with.

e.g. This country is unable to **reach an understanding with** other countries concerning the matter of climate change.

e.g. I was finally able to **reach an understanding with** my neighbor, and now we see eye to eye.

Reach for the sky set high goals.

e.g. **Reach for the sky**, and go for it!

Reach out to: help someone.

e.g. I was glad that you **reached out to** me when I needed it most.

READ

Read between the lines: understand any hidden meaning.

e.g. If you really **read between the lines**, he might be telling you something else.

e.g. To fully understand his instructions, you have to **read between the lines**.

REASON

Reason against: argue against.

e.g. They were trying to **reason against** your proposal.

Reason out: figure out.

e.g. The manager **reasoned out** the problems the company was facing.

Reason with: discuss with.

e.g. I am trying to **reason with** you why you should not marry that guy.

RECKON

Reckon as: consider or perceive as.

e.g. We all **reckon** you **as** our friend.

e.g. They all **reckon** him **as** a constant irritation, and that is why they always stay away from him.

Reckon with: deal with.

e.g. You must learn how to **reckon with** a difficult situation like this.

e.g. As a manager, I have to **reckon with** difficult customers every day.

REFLECT

Reflect on: remember or think about.

e.g. His speech might make you **reflect on** your own childhood.

REIN

Rein in: control.

e.g. I was glad that you **reined in** your hot temper, and did not do anything irrational.

REMAIN

Remain ahead of: stay in front of.

e.g. We were so busy that we could hardly **remain ahead of** the orders we received.

Remain at: stay at.

e.g. Please **remain at** home until I call you.

RESORT

Resort to: turn to something not as the first choice.

e.g. I hope we would not have to **resort to** a lawsuit to settle the matter.

RIP

Rip off: steal something from someone.

e.g. You paid $100 for that! You were **ripped off**!

Rip on: give someone a hard time (slang).

e.g. Don't **rip on** me; I'm your friend!

ROOT

Root for: cheer someone.

e.g. The spectators were **rooting for** the quarter-back.

Root out: remove something

e.g. The Chairman wanted to **root out** all corruption in the company.

RULE

Rule on: give a decision or judgment.

e.g. The Attorney General will have to **rule on** this issue.

Rule out: eliminate.

e.g. I tried to **rule out** all potential dangers.

Rule over: dominate or serve as the boss.

e.g. Don't try to **rule over** me; you're not my boss!

RUN

Run against: compete with.

e.g. I am going to **run against** him in the coming election.

Run away: leave; escape.

e.g. The burglar **ran away** before the police arrived.

Run down: hit with a vehicle; stop functioning.

e.g. The old man was **run down** by the bus.

e.g. My lawn mower is **running down**; I need to get a new one.

Run into: meet by accident

e.g. Yesterday, I **ran into** an old friend that I had not seen for decades.

Run over: come by for a quick visit.

e.g. Can you **run over** for a minute? I've something important to tell you.

Run out of: do not have any more of something

e.g. Hurry! We're **running out of** time!

e.g. He could not make the dessert because he **ran out of** milk and sugar.

"S"

SADDLE

Saddle with: burden someone with.

e.g. I'm sorry I've to **saddle** you **with** taking care of my child.

SAIL

Sail into: attack (figuratively); chastise.

e.g. The angry coach **sailed into** the players in the middle of the game.

e.g. The woman **sailed into** the caretaker for not taking good care of her boy.

SALT

Salt away: put away as reserve.

e.g. We should **salt away** some money in case of emergency.

SAVE

Save for a rainy day: save something for emergency.

e.g. Don't spend all your money; **save** some **for a rainy day**.

SCHOOL

School in: train or discipline.

e.g. The teacher is trying to **school** some of his students **in** discipline.

e.g. You should **school** yourself **in** patience and tolerance.

SCRAPE

Scrape through: barely pass (usually a test).

e.g. I thought I would fail in my math test, but I **scraped through** it.

Scrape up: find or search for.

e.g. I don't know offhand a lawyer who would do your case. See if I could **scrape up** someone later.

SCREW

Screw around with: play around with, usually not doing anything positive (slang).

e.g. Don't **screw around with** that guy and waste your time!

Screw up: mess up; spoil.

e.g. See, you've **screwed up** my plan! I wish you hadn't come.

SEE

See eye to eye: agree about.

e.g. Do you **see eye to eye** with your in-laws about this?

e.g. We never **see eye to eye** with each other; that's why we always argue.

SELL

Sell down the river: betray (slang).

e.g. He is not to be trusted; he's the guy who will **sell** you **down the river**.

Sell out: be sold until there is no more.

e.g. All the boxes were **sold out**; we've no more left. Come back tomorrow.

SEND

Send on a wild-goose chase: send someone looking for something that does not exist.

e.g. Her friends **sent** her **on a wild-goose chase** while preparing a surprise birthday party for her.

SET

Set one back on one's heels: surprise or shock (colloquial).

e.g. His comments **set me back on my heels**, and I was totally dumb-founded.

Set out: leave for a place.

e.g. We'll **set out for** home at dawn tomorrow.

Set the stage for: prepare the way for.

e.g. The President's comments had **set the stage for** more criticism and controversy.

SHOOT

Shoot for the sky: aim very high.

e.g. Don't **shoot for the sky**, or else you may become disappointed.

Shoot one's mouth off: brag or exaggerate about.

e.g. He is always **shooting his mouth off** about his daughter's accomplishments.

SIT

Sit around: relax sitting; waste time sitting.

e.g. Don't just **sit around**; find something to do!

Sit on the fence: be unable to take side, or refuse to choose.

e.g. I will **sit on the fence**, and let you guys decide.

e.g. Whenever it comes to choosing side, he always **sits on the fence**.

Sit up and take notice: be alert and observant.

e.g. You should **sit up and take notice** when the Mayor is going to address the audience.

SLAP

Slap on the wrist: give someone mild punishment.

e.g. You should be glad that your boss only **slapped** you **on the wrist** for the big blunder you made.

SLIM

Slim down: become thinner; lose some weight.

e.g. If you would like to **slim down** a little, give up your favorite dessert.

SLIP

Slip by: (time) pass quickly.

e.g. Time really **slips by**; before you know it, it's almost the end of the year.

Slip up: make an error.

e.g. I'm sorry I **slipped up** again!

SNAP

Snap at: speak angrily and sharply at.

e.g. Don't **snap at** me like that! I was just making a suggestion.

Snap out of: recover or return to normal.

e.g. She had a bad cold, but she quickly **snapped out of** it.

e.g. It was an economic downturn, but the country quickly **snapped out of** it.

SOCK

Sock away: put away something as reserve.

e.g. Fortunately, his wife has **socked** some money **away** every month; now they've something to live on.

SOUP

Soup up: make something more powerful (colloquial).

e.g. The mechanic tried to **soup up** the old car's engine.

SPEAK

Speak off the cuff: give a speech without preparation.

e.g. He is an eloquent speaker; he has the talent to **speak off the cuff**.

Speak out of turn: say something inappropriate or improper.

e.g. She **spoke out of turn** when she mentioned his ex-wife at the wedding party.

Speak up: speak loudly.

e.g. Can you **speak up**? I can't hear you!

SPRING

Spring for: agree to pay or treat.

e.g. My parents have agreed to **spring for** the dinner tonight.

SQUARE

Square off with: prepare for a fight with.

e.g. My brother is going to **square off with** him over this matter.

STAND

Stand by: support.

e.g. Don't worry! I'll always **stand by** you, and you can count on that!

Stand to reason: be reasonable or rational.

e.g. It **stands to reason** that we should pay less tax than those billionaires.

Stand well with: be acceptable to.

e.g. I hope your suggestions will **stand well with** your boss.

STASH

Stash away: hide or put away.

e.g. I always **stash away** some quarters for the parking meter.

STEP

Step down: resign or retire.

e.g. Because of the sex scandal, the CEO had to **step down**.

Step up: increase an activity.

e.g. We hoped the product promotion would **step up** the business, but it didn't.

"T"

TAG

Tag along: go along with.

e.g. We're going to a bar. Do you want to **tag along**?

TAIL

Tail after: follow (colloquial).

e.g. You always **tail after** her wherever she goes.

Tail off: decrease and dwindle to nothing.

e.g. The unemployment rate is now beginning to **tail off**.

TAKE

Take a crack at: make an attempt to.

e.g. She thinks she can do it. Now, she is **taking a crack at** it.

e.g. The man wanted to stop his son from taking drugs, and he **took a crack at** him.

Take exception to: object or disagree.

e.g. I **take exception to** what you just said; I think it was untrue and humiliating.

Take into account: consider important.

e.g. The company will **take into account** your long years of service.

Take one's breath away: astound and surprise.

e.g. Her spectacular performance **took the audience's breath away**.

Take the rap for: take the blame for someone or something one is not responsible for.

e.g. I'm not going to **take the rap for** what you did against my advice.

Take to one's heels: run away.

e.g. As soon as he saw us, he **took to his heels** and was gone.

Take upon oneself: accept the entire burden or responsibility of.

e.g. You don't have to **take all upon yourself** the project we are going to launch; we can help you with that.

TALK

Talk back: answer impolitely.

e.g. It's rude to **talk back** to your parents like that.

Talk over: discuss.

e.g. We'll **talk over** these matters before we see your parents.

Talk up a storm: talk a great deal.

e.g. Whenever I mention this subject, you always **talk up a storm**.

TAPER

Taper off: end gradually; decrease slowly.

e.g. I want to **taper off** my drinking habits.

e.g. Sales usually **taper off** throughout the summer.

TELL

Tell off: dismiss with a scolding.

e.g. I **tell** him **off** whenever he mentions that.

e.g. She was **told off** once and for all.

THINK

Think over: consider.

e.g. The committee **thought over** the proposal and decided against it.

Think through: consider something from beginning to end.

e.g. You have to **think through** the whole procedure to see if you can operate the machine.

Think up: create; invent.

e.g. Can you **think up** an alternative proposal?

THRIVE

Thrive on: grow vigorously because of.

e.g. Children **thrive on** love and attention.

TOUCH

Touch on: mention briefly.

e.g. The professor barely **touched on** the subject of Civil War.

Touch up: repair.

e.g. Can you **touch up** the scratches on the door?

TURN

Turn in: go to bed (colloquial).

e.g. Guys, it's time to **turn in**; it's getting late!

Turn out: attend or appear; end or happen. .

e.g. Many people **turned out** for the meeting.

e.g. The project did not **turn out** as expected: it did not bring in a lot of profit.

Turn up: happen.

e.g. I did not show up at the party because something unexpected had **turned up**.

"U"

URGE

Urge along: encourage someone to continue or go faster.

e.g. He wanted to give up his project, but the manager **urged** him **along** with much encouragement.

"V"

VARY

Vary with: differ from.

e.g. Your figures **vary with** ours considerably. You'd better go back and check them again.

"W"

WAFFLE

Waffle around: be indecisive.

e.g. Make up your mind, and don't **waffle around**!

WAIT

Wait on: serve diligently.

e.g. Do you expect your husband to **wait on** you while you do nothing?

WALK

Walk back: return to where one was.

e.g. We had to **walk back** because we forgot the key.

Walk in on: interrupt by entering.

e.g. I didn't mean to **walk in on** your party; I thought you were all by yourself.

Walk one's feet off: walk too much and become tired.

e.g. I think I've to sit down; I've **walked my feet off** just now.

Walk over: go to where someone is.

e.g. I have something to give to you. Can you **walk over**?

WEAR

Wear out one's welcome: visit too often that one is no longer welcome.

e.g. I don't think we should visit them again this weekend. I don't want to **wear out our welcome**.

e.g. Please come; you won't **wear out your welcome**!

WIND

Wind up: get someone excited (colloquial); end by doing something else.

e.g. This rock music will **wind** the teenagers **up**.

e.g. Instead of going to a movie, they **wound up** in a bar, drinking alcohol.

WIPE

Wipe out: kill; exhaust completely (slang).

e.g. The government was trying to **wipe out** the terrorists.

e.g. The marathon race **wiped** me **out**.

WISE

Wise up to: figure out someone or something.

e.g. It's time you **wise up to** your friend; he is not what you think he is.

e.g. You must **wise up to** how this machine works.

WORK

Work itself out: solve the problem by itself.

e.g. Don't worry; all the problems will **work themselves out**.

Work over: beat someone up (slang).

e.g. If you do this to them, they will **work** you **over**.

"Y"

YEN

Yen for: desire or long for.

e.g. I'm so hungry; I **yen for** a burger!

"Z"

Zero in on: aim directly at.

e.g. I think we should **zero in on** the more important issues first.

ABOUT STEPHEN LAU

About Stephen Lau

http://www.stephencmlau.com

Books by Stephen Lau:

http://www.booksbystephenlau.com

Stephen Lau's Related Blogs:

http://blog-for-esl.blogspot.com/
http://effectivewritingmadesimple.blogspot.com/

Stephen Lau's Related Books:

    Effective Writing Made Simple

    English Slang and Colloquial Expressions for ESL Learners

    English Words and Phrases Frequently Confused and Misused

    Everyday American Idioms for ESL Learners

Contact:

stephencmlau@gmail.com